WHAT DYSLEXIA:

A Parent's Guide to Teaching Kids About Dyslexia

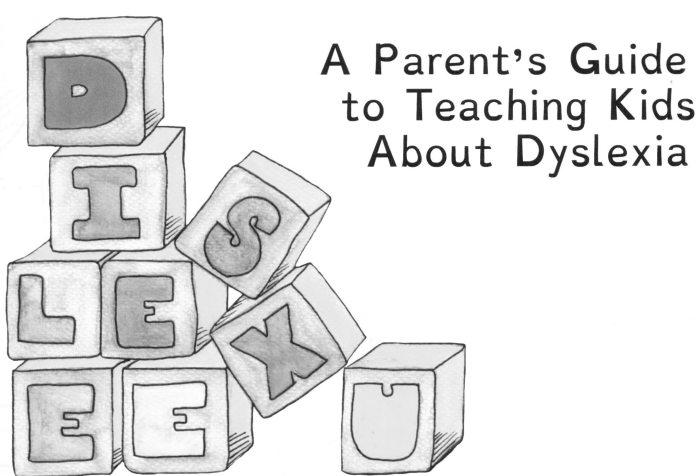

Written by Marianne Sunderland

Illustrated by Laura Mazzello

What is Dyslexia?
A Parent's Guide to Teaching Kids About Dyslexia

HomeschoolingWithDyslexia.com

ISBN-13: 978-1530073283

ISBN-10: 1530073286

Illustrations by Laura Mazzello.

Publishing Services by MelindaMartin.me.

Printed in the United States of America.

This book uses the Dyslexie font from DyslexieFont.com.

WHAT IS DYSLEXIA?

A Parent's Guide to Teaching Kids About Dyslexia

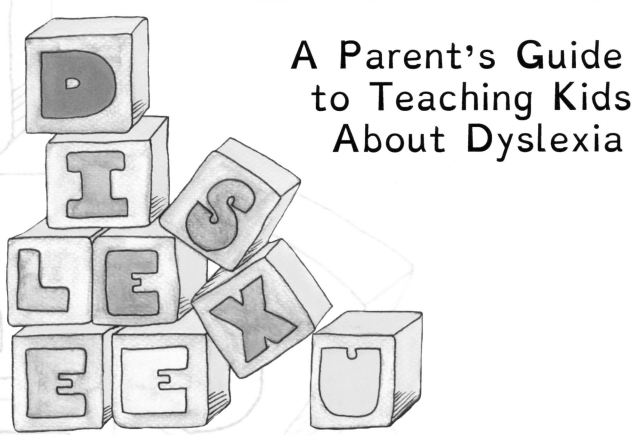

Written by Marianne Sunderland

Illustrated by Laura Mazzello

DEDICATION

To dyslexic kids and adults everywhere who are brilliant but learn differently. May this book help you understand that you have a beautiful brain and much to offer your family, your community and your world.

Why is it important to talk to your kids about dyslexia?

As a long time dyslexia advocate, I talk to a lot of parents about what dyslexia is and how best to parent and educate our kids with this genetic, neurologically-based, language processing phenomenon that is dyslexia. As a mom of 7 kids with dyslexia and the wife of a dyslexic entrepreneur, I have had plenty of opportunity to get to know the many faces of dyslexia.

Most parents of dyslexics agree that, despite their kids' struggles to read, they are smart—really smart.

Most parents of dyslexics will agree that their kids have some amazing talents outside the classroom.

Most parents of dyslexics understand that their role as advocate is critical to their child's success in life.

What many parents do disagree about, however, is *what to tell their kids about their dyslexia.*

Some parents believe that by telling their kids they have dyslexia, their kids will use that knowledge for an excuse not to work hard, possibly resulting in lower ambitions in life.

I get this. Different kids may react differently to this knowledge, but in large part, kids are relieved to know that there is a reason **why** they are struggling. They benefit greatly from the knowledge that they learn *differently* and can begin to look proactively with a positive mindset for ways to enhance their different strengths.

Some parents feel that by telling their kids (and others) about their dyslexia, their kids will be judged by many of the myths surrounding dyslexia. One of these myths, for example, is that kids with dyslexia lack intelligence. Many parents fear that their child will be considered stupid.

The irony of this is that unless a child knows the truth about dyslexia, they will often believe that they aren't as smart as other kids, too.

Some parents fear judgement from others that they themselves are poor parents, that the reason their kids are struggling in school is because they are lazy, not trying or have bad attitudes. This is often referred to as labeling and has a negative connotation that there is something inherently wrong with their kids.

Although I understand this reasoning, I am strongly opposed to it. If we walk around in fear of our kids being misjudged, we miss the bigger issue. As parents of kids with dyslexia, it is our **duty** to inform and educate those that are around us so that the pervasive myths that are so damaging to so many people with dyslexia can be debunked.

Teach them what dyslexia is!

Here's why I believe that we must teach our kids about what dyslexia is (and isn't).

If you have read my book, *Dyslexia 101*, read my blog at homeschoolingwithdyslexia.com or taken one of our parent dyslexia classes, you know that dyslexia affects much more than reading. Dyslexia can also affect spelling, handwriting, math, memory, organization and the ability to focus.

While all kids with dyslexia can learn to read, it is often on a different time table than other kids their ages. Even with proper teaching or tutoring, kids with dyslexia often learn to read and gain fluency later than their peers. Even if they are able to keep up with their peers, they may struggle in other areas.

All this to say that *eventually your child with dyslexia is going to notice that there is something different about them*. They are going to begin to wonder if they are actually smart.

Some parents are afraid to tell their kids about their dyslexia because they afraid to hurt their self-confidence. In fact, it is quite the opposite.

I've talked to many dyslexic adults about their experiences growing up. If they didn't know that their learning struggles were caused by a genetic brain-wiring difference, they usually ended up doubting their intelligence and suffering anxiety and a major loss of confidence.

Compare this with the child who is struggling in their studies who is told the truth about dyslexia:

- It is genetic.

- Their mom or dad or aunt or uncle or grandparent was likely dyslexic and passed it on to them.

- Pretty much every dyslexic has average (and many have above average) intelligence.

- They learn differently.

We should also be teaching them about the *many distinct strengths* of the dyslexic brain-wiring.

Has your husband or one of your older children ever come home late from work or a night out with friends? As we begin to wonder where they are, our ideas of what may have happened to them begin to form. It's human nature to fill in information voids with worst-case scenarios.

Ironically, when parents keep their kids' dyslexia a secret to protect them, it can often lead to fear and shame. Fear can keep kids from getting the help they need in the form of, first, remediation, and eventually, accommodations.

We must also understand that dyslexia is not outgrown. While the struggles change as our kids grow up, the need is still there for support. For example, decoding words and spelling are the main problems in the early school years, keeping up with the sheer volume of reading and writing in middle and high school. Kids with dyslexia need the support of their teachers to help them achieve their full intellectual potential despite their struggles with the written word.

How much better would it be for a student's learning struggles to be defined and discussed with teachers? Instead of worrying about what everyone will think, share the information with those involved in the education of your children so that an appropriate academic plan can be developed to help minimize their weaknesses and maximize their strengths.

How To Use This Book

What is Dyslexia? A Parent's Guide to Teaching Kids About Dyslexia is the perfect tool to begin the conversation with your student or child about his or her dyslexia. It is intentionally simple. Concepts are kept clear and to the point and are meant to lay a foundation for understanding dyslexia—both the strengths and weaknesses.

As you read, stop and ask questions. Ask about their feelings or where they perceive their strengths to be. Some examples are, "Can you name 3 things that you are good at? Not just in school but anywhere. Are you good at sports? Do you love caring for animals? Are you a good cook? Maybe you're the friendly kid who knows everyone. Can you tell good jokes? Are you a good brother or sister?"

Remind them that it is hard work to learn to read and spell but that they will learn these things!

Refer back to the ideas in the book often. Teaching kids about the many facets of dyslexia and their own unique dyslexia strengths and weaknesses is an ongoing process that will result in a young adult fully capable of advocating for themselves in the world.

More Tips For Parents

Getting a dyslexia diagnosis can be overwhelming at first. Accepting that fact will require parents to get educated on what dyslexia is so that they can become their child's advocate and thereby teach them over time to become their own advocates.

Talk To Your Kids

Talk to your kids about what dyslexia is and isn't. This isn't a one-time conversation but rather an ongoing discussion. All kids will have trouble in one area or another.

Help Them To Find Their Gifts And Talents

It doesn't matter what it is as long as it is an arena where your child can feel victorious, develop confidence and not feel like he or she is the one always struggling to catch up.

Get Them The Appropriate Help

All people with dyslexia can learn to read with the right methods. Parents can teach their kids at home using an Orton-Gillingham based reading program or by hiring a certified dyslexia tutor.

Read To Your Kids

Some of the many benefits of reading out loud are to help increase vocabulary, base knowledge and to develop and strengthen a love for reading.

Get Audio Books

Available on **CD**s or digital downloads, audio books are a great way to, as **Ben Foss** says, "ear read" books at their intellectual level that they may not be able to read on their own yet.

Help When Needed

If your kids are studying a particular subject, you can help them by learning alongside them. **G**et books or **DVD**s from the library to supplement what they are learning.

Acknowledge Effort

Praise for process or effort is one of the most powerful things a parent or teacher can do to motivate a child to keep trying. **N**ote that we are not praising performance which might be poor despite the effort.

Teach Perseverance

Kids with dyslexia will need to work harder. It is going to take more time and effort for them to read, and we need to teach our kids to be strong. This is best learned by example.

Communicate With Teachers

You are your child's advocate and by doing so will be teaching them to eventually advocate for themselves. Know their diagnosis, know their strengths, know their weaknesses and know what they need for accommodations in the classroom to be successful.

Lastly

Self-image is formed by the age of 10. Successful dyslexics say that the top 3 things that affected them for success are:

1. Parent Or Teacher Support And Encouragement

Listen to your child as they talk about their feelings. They can have trouble expressing themselves so step back and allow them to take the time to find the words. Gently ask questions and wait patiently for a response. Reward effort not product. For the dyslexic, grades should be less important than progress.

2. Finding An Area In Which He Or She Could Succeed

In some cases, the strengths are obvious and in others they are more subtle. Hone in on your child's interests and help them to find meaningful experiences involving them.

3. Developing A Commitment To Helping Others

They may do volunteer work for charities or churches or choose vocations that require empathy. These experiences help dyslexics to feel more positive about themselves and deal more effectively with their own pain and struggles. Other opportunities exist in schools, homes and churches for dyslexics to help others. Even tutoring or reading to younger dyslexic students and being able to encourage them can help them feel better about themselves.

THINGS YOU NEED TO KNOW ABOUT DYSLEXIA

Dyslexia is just a big word to explain why some people find it unusually hard to learn to read, write and spell.

You are smart!

People with dyslexia are smart but
have trouble learning to
read and spell.

Some people learn best with
words; other people learn best with
pictures and ideas.

Dyslexia is genetic.

Just like you get your
hair and eye color from your
parents or grandparents,
you got your dyslexia from
one of them as well.

That means that
dyslexia is not a mistake—
it is simply how God made you!

People with dyslexia are smart but learn differently so they need to be taught differently.

Once your parents and teachers know that you are dyslexic, they can teach you in the ways that you learn best.

Lots of people are dyslexic.

1 out of every 5 kids
(and adults) are dyslexic.

You will learn to read,
but it will take hard work.

Sometimes it can seem like
you'll never be a good reader,
but you will!

THINGS THAT CAN BE HARD FOR PEOPLE WITH DYSLEXIA

Some kids with dyslexia
also have trouble with math,
especially memorizing math facts.

People with dyslexia are
good at understanding big ideas.

On the other hand, they're not so
good at remembering little ideas
and details like math facts.

Some kids with dyslexia have
trouble with things like
tidying their toys and clothes,
keeping their rooms clean or
organizing their backpacks
and other belongings.

When talking with other people, some kids with dyslexia have trouble finding just the right word to say what they mean or don't understand jokes quickly.

WHAT IT CAN FEEL LIKE
TO BE DYSLEXIC

Being dyslexic can be
frustrating while you are
learning to read and spell.

That is completely normal.

Everyone gets frustrated by doing
things that are hard.

People who don't give up soon
learn that they can do anything.
You can, too!

Sometimes your parents
or teachers may think
you're not trying hard enough.

They probably don't realize that
you are working
extra hard!

It's no fun being misunderstood, but
it happens to everyone sometimes.

When other people find out that you aren't as good a reader as they are, it can be embarrassing.

You may feel anxious or nervous, especially when you are asked to read in front of people.

You can tell your teachers and friends that you are dyslexic to help them understand.

Sometimes you may feel
angry or discouraged by the
things that you can't do well.

Let's take a look at the things that
you are good at!

COOL THINGS PEOPLE WITH DYSLEXIA CAN DO

Some people with dyslexia
have the ability to think in pictures,
kind of like a movie playing in their
heads.

This means that they are
often good at making art,
understanding science, engineering
or building and designing things,
and inventing new things that have
never been made before!

People with dyslexia are very good problem solvers.

Many start their own businesses and are very successful.

They can think of better ways to do things probably because of their dyslexia.

People with dyslexia are often very good with people.

They are known for their kindness and make the very best of friends.

They often like to help others.

People with dyslexia are
often very creative.

Many dyslexic people are employed
as designers, artists, actors and
chefs.

People with dyslexia are often very good at sports.

There are many famous athletes with dyslexia such as football player Tim Tebow, basketball player Magic Johnson, baseball player Nolan Ryan and Olympic runner Carl Lewis.

People with dyslexia have a hard
time with some things, but they
also have a wide variety
of skills and talents.

Keep trying, and know that one day
you will read and write and spell
and do great things!

About the Author

Marianne Sunderland has been homeschooling her 8 children, 7 of whom are dyslexic, since 1996. Despite a rich educational experience of travel and individualized teaching, her oldest child, though obviously very bright, struggled mysteriously to crack the code of reading.

Educational testing revealed dyslexia.

An educated parent and avid reader, Marianne knew that without a strong foundation in reading skills, her son would struggle in all areas of his life and future education.

There were many days of tears and exasperation as Marianne tried one thing after another to teach her bright but struggling kids. She understands how it feels to be completely overwhelmed and frustrated by the load of information (and misinformation) about dyslexia that exists today.

Years later and after becoming a trained Orton-Gillingham dyslexia tutor, she has been able to successfully teach her children with dyslexia using individualized, multi-sensory and research-based methods.

It has become Marianne's mission to help others get educated about dyslexia and to know that all people with dyslexia can learn to read, write and spell with the right methods!

She is the creator of HomeschoolingWithDyslexia.com, a site dedicated to educating and encouraging parents to successfully teach and advocate for their children with dyslexia.

She is also a popular speaker, homeschool consultant, certified Orton-Gillingham tutor and author of *Dyslexia 101: Truths, Myths and What Really Works*, a parent's guide to navigating the world of dyslexia.

For more information, visit:

HomeschoolingWithDyslexia.com